# Day and Night

Anita Ganeri

 **www.heinemann.co.uk/library**
Visit our website to find out more information about **Heinemann Library** books.

To order:
- Phone 44 (0) 1865 888066
- Send a fax to 44 (0) 1865 314091
- Visit the Heinemann Bookshop at www.heinemann.co.uk/library to browse our catalogue and order online.

First published in Great Britain by Heinemann Library, Halley Court, Jordan Hill, Oxford OX2 8EJ, part of Harcourt Education. Heinemann is a registered trademark of Harcourt Education Ltd.



Editorial: Jilly Attwood, Kate Bellamy
Design: Jo Hinton-Malivoire
Picture research: Ginny Stroud-Lewis, Ruth Blair
Production: Séverine Ribierre

Originated by Ambassador Litho Ltd
Printed and bound in China by South China Printing Company

ISBN 0 431 11397 1 (hardback)
08 07 06 05 04
10 9 8 7 6 5 4 3 2 1

ISBN 0 431 11403 X (paperback)
08 07 06 05
10 9 8 7 6 5 4 3 2 1

**British Library Cataloguing in Publication Data**
Ganeri, Anita
Day and Night - (Nature's Patterns)
529.1
A full catalogue record for this book is available from the British Library.

**Acknowledgements**
The Publishers would like to thank the following for permission to reproduce photographs: Alamy pp. **12**, **13**; Alamy p. **14** (Worldwide Picture Library); Ardea p. **29;** Corbis pp. **20** (Paul Barton), **27** (Eric and David Hosking), **17** (Rob Matheson), **19** (Roger Ressmeyer), **8**, **21** (Royalty Free), **28** (Bill Stormont), **10** (Jeff Vanuga); Getty Images p. **9** (Brank X Pictures); Getty Images/Photodisc pp. **4**, **5**, **7**, **15**, **16**, **18**, **22**; Harcourt Index p. **30**; Image Bank p. **26**; Martin Soukias p. **23**; Science Photo Library pp. **24**, **25**.

Cover photograph of Sydney is reproduced with permission of Lonely Planet Images/Mark Kirby.

Our thanks to David Lewin for his assistance in the preparation of this book.



The paper used to print this book comes from sustainable resources.

# Contents



Words appearing in the text in bold, **like this**, are explained in the Glossary.

Find out more about Nature's Patterns at www.heinemannexplore.co.uk

# Nature's patterns

Nature is always changing. Many of the changes that happen follow a **pattern**. This means that they happen over and over again.

*The day is light. This side of the Earth is facing the Sun.*

Day and night follow a pattern. Every morning, it gets light and the day begins. Every evening, it gets dark and we have night. Then day starts all over again.

# Day and night

The Sun **shines** onto the side of the Earth that faces it. This side is light and has day. The other side is dark and has night.

*The light side of the Earth has day. The dark side has night.*

It is daytime on this side of the Earth.

The Earth is always **spinning** round. So places on the Earth go in and out of the sunlight. This is why day changes into night.

# Light and dark

During the day, most of our light comes from the Sun. It comes in **rays** that travel in straight lines. We need light to see things.

*The Sun shines down on the Earth from space.*

At night, the place where you live is dark because it faces away from the Sun. We have to make our own light to see at night.

# Sunrise

Every morning, the Sun **rises** in the sky. This is called **sunrise** and it is when daytime begins.

*Sunrise is sometimes called dawn.*

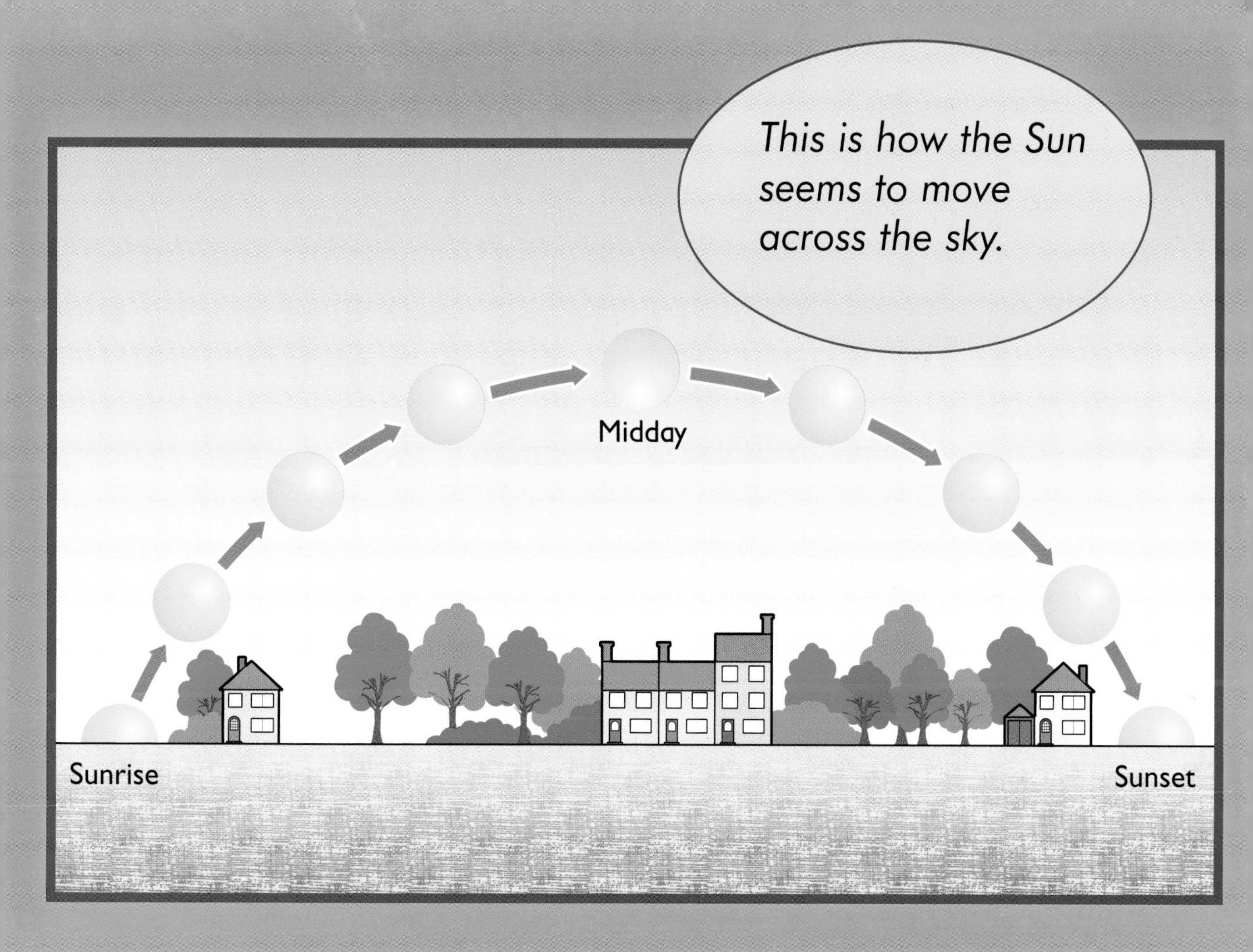


We can see the Sun travel across the sky in the day. But the Sun is not moving. It seems to move because of the way the Earth is **spinning**.

# Midday

At 12 o'clock, it is **midday**. At midday, the Sun is high up in the sky. This is usually the hottest time of the day.

*The hot midday Sun heats up the ground.*

On a sunny day, you can see your **shadow**. It follows you everywhere. Your shadow changes length during the day. It is very short at midday.

# Sunset

Every evening, the Sun starts to get lower, or set, in the sky. This is called **sunset** and it is when night begins.

*Sunset is sometimes called dusk.*

At sunset, there is less and less light. The sky slowly gets darker. It does not go dark suddenly like switching off a light.

*At dusk it starts to get dark because the Sun is setting.*

# The Moon

At night, you can see the Moon in the sky. The Moon is there in the daytime, too. But you can see it better in the dark.

*You can see the Moon because sunlight bounces off it.*

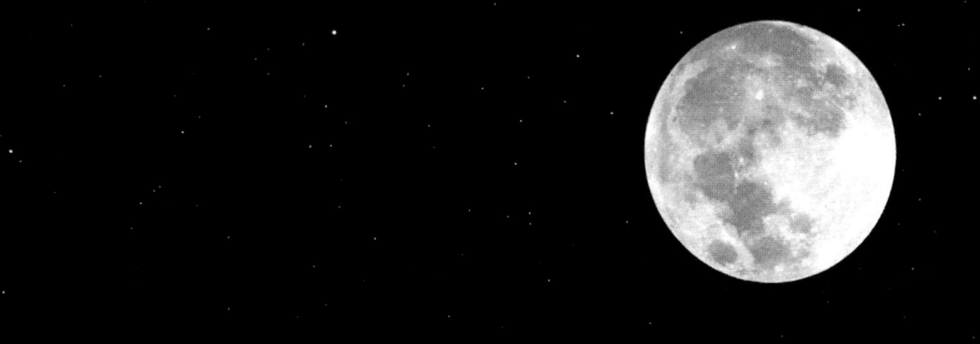

*This is a full Moon. You can see all of the bright side.*

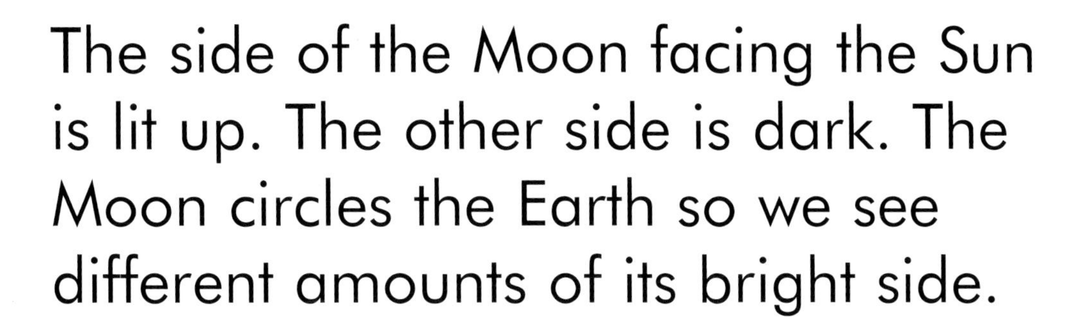

The side of the Moon facing the Sun is lit up. The other side is dark. The Moon circles the Earth so we see different amounts of its bright side.

# Starry night

The stars you can see at night are like our Sun. They look like tiny dots of light because they are so far away.

*Can you see the stars on a dark night?*

In the daytime, you cannot see the stars because the Sun's light is too strong. At night, they seem to shine brightly because the sky is dark.

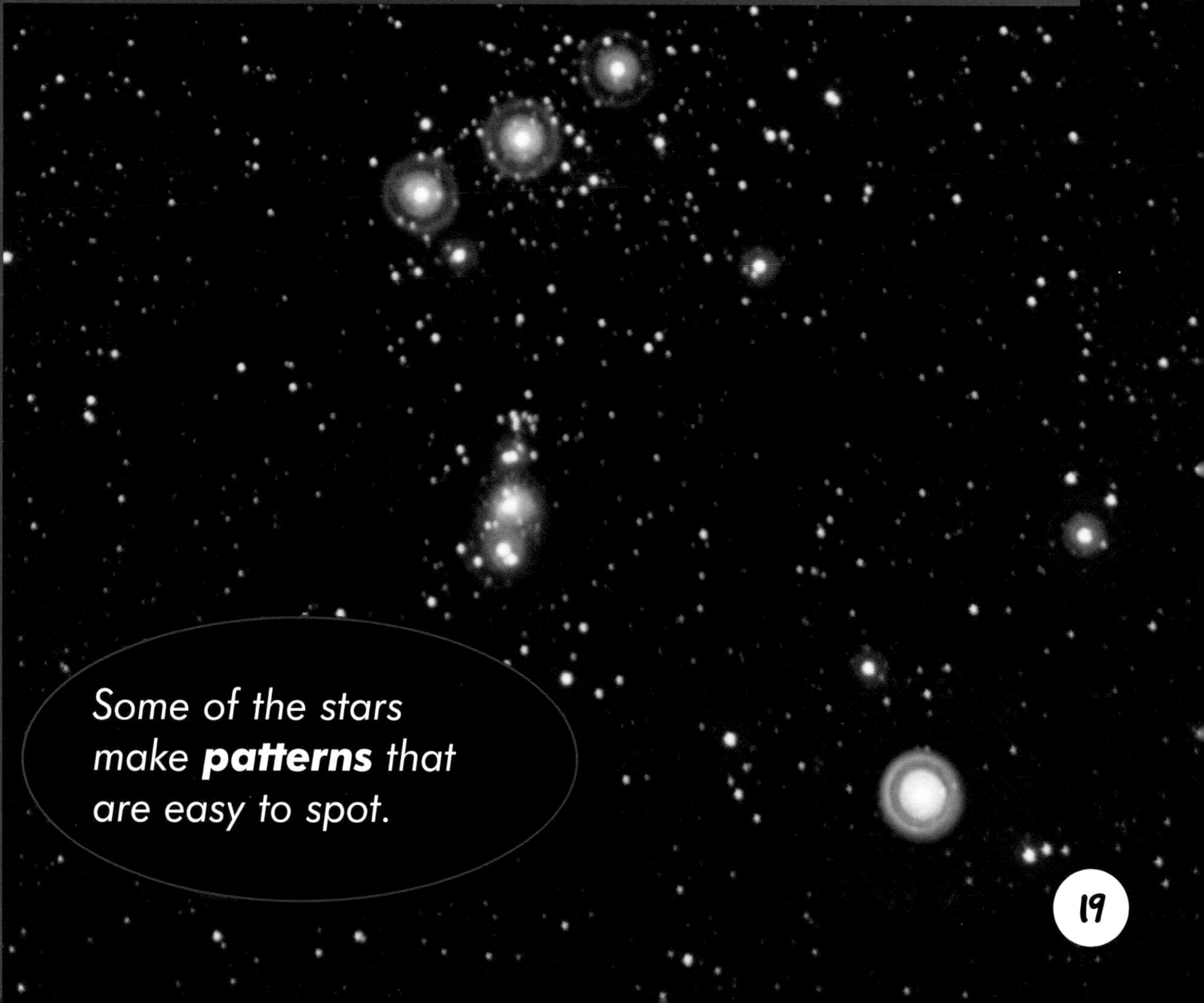

*Some of the stars make **patterns** that are easy to spot.*

# Around the world

Different parts of the world have day and night at different times. When it is getting light in one place, it is getting dark somewhere else.

This is because half of the Earth faces away from the Sun and is in shadow. As the Earth spins, places come out of the shadow into daylight.

# Dates and times

A whole day is 24 hours long. This is how long it takes the Earth to spin round once. We divide this up into day and night.

These clocks show what time it is in different parts of the world.

We use watches and clocks to tell us what time of day or night it is. Calendars help us to measure the days, weeks and months.

# Plants by day and night

Some plants can tell when it is day or night. They open their flowers during the day for insects to visit.

*Plants need sunlight to make their food and grow.*

At night, the insects go back to their nests. Then the plants close up their flowers. Next morning, they open them up again to face the Sun.

*This flower has closed its petals for the night.*

# Out in the day

Most people work in the day when it is light. Farmers start work outside as soon as it gets light. They often stop work when it gets dark.

*A farmer's day starts early as it is getting light.*

Many animals are also busy during the daytime. The animals they eat are out too, so they are easier to catch.

*After its bath, this bird will dry its feathers in the Sun.*

# Out at night

Some people work at night when everyone else is asleep. Fire fighters may be called out to fight a fire in the middle of the night.

*People that work at night have to sleep in the day.*

Some animals sleep in the day. At night they **hunt** for food. Cats can see well in the dark because their eyes open wide to let light in.

*Cats also use their whiskers to help them feel their way in the dark.*

# Phases of the Moon

The Moon circles around the Earth. As the Moon moves, it seems to change shape in the sky. The different shapes are called phases. The phases of the Moon form a **pattern** that happens over and over again.

new moon

crescent moon

half moon

full moon



Find out more about Nature's Patterns at www.heinemannexplore.co.uk

# Glossary

**hunt** look for and catch animals to eat

**midday** the middle of the day at 12 o'clock. Midday is also called noon.

**pattern** something that happens over and over again

**rays** straight lines of sunlight

**rises** goes up

**shadow** a dark patch made when an object blocks out the Sun's light

**shines** gives off light

**spinning** turning round and round

**sunrise** the early morning when the Sun rises in the sky

**sunset** the evening when the Sun sinks, or sets, in the sky

# More books to read

*Space Explorer: The Moon,* Patricia Whitehouse (Heinemann Library, 2004)

*Space Explorer: The Sun,* Patricia Whitehouse (Heinemann Library, 2004)

*Why is Night Dark?,* Sophy Tahta (Usborne Publishing, 2002)

# Index